# SCATTERED LIGHT

# JEREMY HOOKER

# SCATTERED LIGHT

ENITHARMON PRESS

First published in 2015
by Enitharmon Press
10 Bury Place
London WC1A 2JL

www.enitharmon.co.uk

Distributed in the UK by
Central Books
99 Wallis Road
London E9 5LN

Distributed in the USA and Canada
by Independent Publishers Group
814 North Franklin Street
Chicago, IL 60610
USA
www.ipgbook.com

ISBN: 978-1-910392-08-9

Enitharmon Press gratefully acknowledges the financial support of
Arts Council England, through Grants for the Arts.

Individuals contribute to sustain the Press through the
Enitharmon Friends Scheme. We are deeply grateful to all Friends,
particularly our Patrons: Colin Beer, Sean O'Connor and those
who wished to remain anonymous.

British Library Cataloguing-in-Publication Data.
A catalogue record for this book is available
from the British Library.

Designed in Albertina by Libanus Press
and printed in England by
Short Run Press

In memory of Anne Cluysenaar

# ACKNOWLEDGEMENTS

I wish to express my thanks to the editors and publishers of the following publications in which some of these poems first appeared, sometimes in earlier versions: *Agenda, English, Images of Warsash and the Hamble River 1790–2009, London Magazine, New Welsh Review, Planet, Plant Care: A Festschrift for Mimi Khalvati, P.N. Review, Poetry Wales, A Room to Live In: A Kettle's Yard Anthology, Scintilla, Shearsman, 10th Muse, The Lampeter Journal, The Powys Journal, Times Literary Supplement*. 'Butterfly extravaganza' was broadcast on BBC Radio 3.

I am indebted to Jude James's *Hurst Castle: An Illustrated History* (The Dovecote Press, 1986) for some historical detail used in 'Hurst Castle'.

I am grateful to Literature Wales for a Writer's Bursary that enabled me to complete the collection of poems.

# CONTENTS

# 1 BROTHER WORM

## BROTHER WORM

1

One moment in Valdivia
when the ground under him rocked
he learnt that land also is a sea.

One moment is enough:
no security can hold.
From high to low,
all that was immutable shifts.

Along the coast, in Quiriquina,
at Concepcion, it was as though
a fleet had been wrecked – timbers
that were roofs, furniture, smashed,
strewn on the beach, storehouses
burst open, merchandise scattered,
rocks, even rocks, torn from the deep.

Far from home
the ground moving from under him
like the *Beagle* in a cross ripple,
or more like ice, thin ice, that bends
under the body's weight.
How describe the sense of it, the world
that stood for all that was solid,
in a moment, gone . . .
                              as an earthworm
through its skin knows vibrations
of mole's snout, or bird above,
beak striking down.

2

He has read the runes –
nothing magical, only
the commonest unnoticed
evidence – castings,
half-decayed leaves
dragged down, inches
of black mould
accumulating.
                    At night
on the lawn at Down,
he has gone with a lantern,
seeking to know
with vibrations and light
the mould-maker.
Indoors, on the piano,
he has worms in a pot
of earth, and plays to them.
Also with a bassoon,
and whistle. And with his breath
which they feel only
when he breathes hard.
Blind, deaf creatures,
how alive they are,
how sensitive,
sifting the soil, burying
and inadvertently
preserving monolith,

atrium, tessellated aisle,
accumulating over
millions of years mould
that bears crops, as he
in a lifetime gathers
facts. Pertinacious man,
who recognises under his feet
a fellow voyager, another
with presence of mind,
adapted to the world
it moves in.
Such are the powers
beneath notice, one
observed that steadies
the observer, makes possible
also the unsteady world
in which he moves,
breathing through the skin.

# 2 UNFINISHED PORTRAITS

## FATHER, PAINTING

What does he see now
as he stands back from the canvas
or bends forward, applying
paint, wielding the palette knife?

How often I have watched him
at his work, just so, but now,
almost blind, ruining a painting
he thinks he is improving.

What do I see, as I sit at my desk
looking down at him – the man
with a brush, the painter with his head
full of colours, and on the easel
where a good painting was, a mess?

The work he is destroying is one
I love – a painting of the Common.

In this, as summer colours
deepen, you can smell the warmth,
and hear pods bursting on the furze,
sense the lizard sunning
on a sandy stone. Gold blazes
in the darkening green. Beyond,
the Island downs – a cool, blue dome.

No one can stop him, or should try.
It is his work to do with as he pleases.
And what he pleases is to see
behind his eyes the deeper tones,
and add, just so, the brighter touch.

## LIEFJE

A scrap of life, but,
awake, she fills the room —
ears back owlishly, paws
off the ground, dancing
on her tail, or flying
through the air sideways.

Asleep in a corner,
the house curls around her
with a mind of its own

dreaming of cat.


## WITH A CAT ON MY SHOULDER

Forgive me, Liefje,
this isn't about you.
It was the feel of your fur
against my neck that brought back
my mother's words: 'he loved cats,
my grandfather, always
had a cat on his shoulder.'
And there he was, an old man
I had never seen before,
feeling with pleasure
a cat asleep against his neck.

## AN UNFINISHED PORTRAIT

*In memory of Gerard Casey*

A card fell out of the book
when I picked it up –
the writing on the back in red ink
unmistakable, though a scrawl
written as your sight failed.

That time it was Dürer,
*The Great Piece of Turf* –
                    you always knew
which image to choose, one
that would speak for you
beyond the reach of words.

What a wonder of definition,
each grass blade, each flower,
each leaf, the dandelions
unopened, all distinct –

earth as never seen before,
vibrant with the breath
of the creator.

Look: we can almost see

*

If I were to return to the room
I would expect to find you there.

Your room, with the presence
of the family around you.

Will and Gertrude in their paintings
on canvas or stones from Chesil Beach.

Theodore and John Cowper in their books.

Mary and Lucy, everywhere –
                'there's more poetry
in Mary's little finger
than in my whole body.'

                It wasn't true,
only you honoured her gift
more than your own.
And when she died, lived
more than half in the other world.

Yet always, when I came away
from seeing you the earth felt
earthier, the Dorset lanes
deeper, and for a long time I too
was no longer travelling
over the surface, but found myself
in touch with a depth
that must be truly the world.

*

Once I found you in the back room
in half-light, an old man
lying under a green blanket.

Canvases glowed on the walls.
Will's African landscapes,

painted when he was an old man
and you had to support his hands
placing your wrists crosswise
beneath them.
               And so he painted
the great space you both loved –
the plains and distant mountains –
that seemed now to surround us
in the small dark room, glowing
as the day darkened.


               Spaces of the great earth
under the sun, and, in a corner,
the corpse of a zebra,
striped skin over bones –
the creature for which,
you said lightly,
you felt an affinity.

*


How could I do you justice
even if I dared to try?

How could anyone?

You who lived in the presence
of divine judgement.
'God reveals to us just what we are.'

And so you accepted to be seen,
as you could not see yourself.

*

Images come back easily.

A strong man walking slowly,
pausing to speak, slowly,
listening, moving on, pausing . . .

A quiet man raising his voice
suddenly, stunning the room
with a sermon, and, afterwards,
saying sorry, without taking back a word.

A man walking on Chesil Beach
scattering ashes,
where his too are scattered now.

*

He would quote Boehme,
'the great deeps of this world'.

In the light of unknowing
every possible end is a beginning,
every image is a rock to break open
in search of the mica sparkle
which at once dulls, if found.

Consider waves breaking on Chesil Beach,
stones in sunlit spray gleaming.

Imagine a man seated alone
in Mappowder church
contemplating the unknowable.

## FOR RAY KLIMEK, PHOTOGRAPHER

Cwm Bargoed, Blaenafon, Treorchy.

The man from Pennsylvania looks about him.

The unimaginable is what he sees with a stranger's eye –
lives made shaping and reshaping
material ground, driving histories
through carboniferous bedrock
and geological process,
being wasted and making waste.

Dust in the lungs and in the eyes,
a landscape of dust,
where the man with a stranger's eye
reveals play of colours –
greens, grey, black –
and textures, shapes, rhythms
of shouldering hills,
fossilised traces of power
in gullies & washeries, tips & lagoons.

Out of the dust he brings to light
tyre tracks, footprints, cloud,
landscapes in flux
uncertain with becoming.

Out of the dust the day's light.
At Cwm Bargoed a wheelbarrow
beside a drainage channel,
dull red, but an ember
against dust-grey slopes.

How small it is, under a hill
the hands that wielded it helped to make –

monumental scarred ground
the stranger's eye discloses, alighting
on dust that was muscle and blood,
on grass that is flesh,

on a new day's uncertain beginning.

# HOMAGE TO ERNEST ZOBOLE

*for Ceri Thomas*

## 1  BLACK VALLEY

He stands in the doorway.

He looks round corners.

He reads lights and stars.

He belongs as much as a dog
nosing in corners.

He is a stranger.

Sensation was his teacher.
Knowledge on fingertips.
A taste on the tongue –

Black rain,
soot-fall light.

Black that reaches into everything.
Black that is a fount of colour.

## 2  IN AND OUT OF THE FRAME

He was everywhere and nowhere –
earthbound and aerial,
prisoner and free man,
man and ghost.

Look and you can imagine him flying,
or see him stretched out, a corpse in the street.

He stands in the doorway
mixing fact with dream.

Forget views – the painting
is the place, the painter
is the place that made him.

### 3 NOCTURNE

Blue was the space he moved in

Blue was what the jackdaws saw
what the dogs sniffed in terrace corners

Blue the bruised and wounded flesh
the seams and masked faces

Blue the unseen

Blue the sea and the freighted ships
Blue the night-sky where the little yellow stars were

Blue the river and the shadowed valley
Blue the windows with a splash of yellow

Blue the taste of the Welsh rain

Blue was the journey that had taken him a lifetime

## POET AMONG FERNS

*In memory of Tony Conran*

1

Gift-giver,
what shall we give you?

What do you need
except to give – at home
in the reception of friends,
among compatriots?

2

I think of you among ferns,
poet with a fernery –

plants of marginal places,
the tough, the delicate,

in crevices in castle walls,
on mountain rock-fall,

ferns following streams
or deep in woodland -

a whole country of ferns
and you their poet.

3

Maidenhair
Lady fern
Hart's-tongue
Spleenwort
Horsetails
of the coal deposits

Bracken with creeping rhizomes,
a life-history underground,
the air rich with spores –
ferns that have mastered the margins,
a whole country of ferns.

4

Once, over head in bracken,
I found myself lost
yards from a country lane,
but lost, briefly in panic.
And what is one loss
but taste of the final loss –
poet with nothing to sell
but himself, some
poor notion of self,
alone and fearful of death?

5

Loneliness was the place
you came in from.

Out of the margins you came
to Wales and a home
on the March between languages.

And what you built there
became a place others could enter,
knowing ground underfoot,
the rich moulds, the life
of leaf-fall, the air
quick with spores:

a place for
'the whole body, the whole mind'.

6

You know the way of the elegies:
mourning in the hall with black hearth,
lament of oak trees in the storm
that racks their limbs,
a tribe undone, bridge over the flood
smashed to matchstick.

These are not for you.
Rather a word of triumph,
a boast, if you like, a brag
of Conran the poet.

But if a brag, a quiet one,
a word befitting a poet walking away
on the path he has given us,
some word tough yet delicate,
true to a country of ferns.

# AT SALTERNS: A MEMORY OF MARY BUTTS

1

No fossil world –

white walls,
domestic land
where furze grew wild,
and she – Blake's daughter – played.

White walls,
the days behind the day
blanked out, her passion
of possession gone.

But what is memory?

2

A fire that's autumn
in the light,
quick dartings in the trees,
a bird, a leaf, a word.

3

So much remains –
beech & conifer,
a glimpse of harbour water
and the distant Purbeck hills –
so much is changed.

But who can stop the passion
once released?

Each garden well an oracle.
Each tree the Tree of Life.

# A WORD FOR DEREK JARMAN

'As a nine-year old on the cliffs at Hordle
I discovered a bank of sweet violets and used to creep
through the hedge that enclosed the school playing field
and lie in the sun dreaming.
What did I dream of in my violet youth?'
        Derek Jarman, *Chroma*


A word for you, glittering man;
but what word, lover in life and dying
of shingle at the land's edge?

A word, maybe, of the cliffs where you dreamed,
cliffs which I climbed, scrambling, sliding
on iron-tinted gravel and sand,
or over which, on the top deck of the bus
to and from school, I looked at the sea
and the chalk skull of West Wight, dreaming . . .

What did we dream of then? For me,
fishing from the beach with a home-made
bamboo rod, casting over the surf.
Fishing, and girls; but most of all fishing.
And nothing beyond the day.

We might have met, streams
before they diverged, different desires
shaping our courses; were, perhaps,
in the same place at the same time
without meeting. And would have shared
a love of Hordle cliffs, of West Wight,
the Needles and the sea. A love too
of lying alone in some enclosed place.

And maybe that would have been all
though I call it much: warmth
of the body pressed among grass like a hare
in its form, sun warm on closed eyes,
sea below whispering, grating gently on shingle,
the expanse of the bay marked by a ship
or a sail, but with a delicious emptiness
some dream could expand to fill,
or fade in the warmth, the scents
of sweetness and salt, the sound
of the sea hushing on shingle, whispering.

# MATHIAS COUNTRY

*In memory of Roland Mathias*

1

He will have imagined it like this:
cloud shadow on Brecon Beacons,
above a drowned valley
that was once home ground.

He will have stood looking down,
or come like a shadow on the water,
leaden and silvery, with a blade of light.

He will not have stopped at the soil
freshly turned among
older burials inside the chapel wall.

He will have looked death in the face,
knowing what he could not know.

2

Who knows this place as he did?

Family histories inscribed on stones,
marks weathered, marks erased
but held in his mind,
remembrancer,
poet of this country.

A book is closed here,
the pages closely written in his hand.

And who will read, who will care
to read with the care he showed,

this teacher, this scholar
of the dark and luminous word,
raiser of buried lives?

3

And he called himself a stranger,
a man standing with his face at the door
of a great house, looking in
at a life he would claim no part of,
thinking himself
unworthy to step inside.

At Aber, among his kin,
he waits for a judgement
no man can make.

But what we can say is this:
here, under sun-struck cloud
and shadow of the Beacons,
above the valley of the Usk,
the man who loved
and remembered has come home.

# MOSAICS

## 1 THE CHRIST OF HINTON ST MARY

How long he lay buried
in Blackmoor fields

his face concealed
under human feet
and hooves of beasts

And was uncovered,
soil brushed from his eyes
so that we may look at him
asking who he is.

And he looks back
returning the question.

Does the chi-rho give him away?
Is the power of his steady gaze
an emperor's fantasy?

Or maybe he has usurped
Bacchus, or followed
in the footsteps of Orpheus,
and returns with the bride.

Unmistakeably a god
shaped in the image of man,
he brings pomegranates,
full-globed, honeycombed
with red seed.

They have lain with him

through hundreds of years,
buried in Blackmoor fields.

## 2  THE MASTER OF THE ACTAEON MOSAIC

Imagine him arranging the pieces,
assembling the design, fingers
growing a skin that is strange to him.
His days too are pieces now,
each a jagged tessera,
which he places, fits, designing
a picture that tells the story
of a young man who entered a place
forbidden to men,
and paid for his trespass.

Quickly death came to him,
he thinks, but not quick enough:
torn by his own hounds, shredded
by slavering jaws.

Imagine: piece by piece
he assembles him, the youth
with hair grown to fur, skin
the flesh of a stag, hands
and feet hooves, that speed
over the ground – too slow
for the dogs – his dogs –
his named dogs, that do not hear,
but fasten their teeth in his neck,
his sides, and tear him

      piece by piece

which he forms, assembles,
as days come and go, each
a jagged tessera, a fragment
of the same story, as he works
in the cursed land, fingers
growing to skin that is strange to him,
far from the field of Mars
and healing power of the Roman sun.

# 3 SCATTERED LIGHT

## LIKE THISTLEDOWN

As a word surprises you
sprung from the language net
drifting across the mind

you don't know where it came from
you don't know what will come of it

but there it is, floating down
or, though you felt no breeze
flying up rapidly
                    out of sight

a winged seed
with connections whose beginning and end
you can only guess at

which may catch on a bird's wing
or land where in time
it will lift a paving-stone

or, like a word no one receives,
drop in a web, like a spider,

        a dead spider.

RAIN

Dark-pitted dust
after drought

Fresh and sweet
on your lips

The word

rain

## MOTHER OF THE WINDS

Sprung from her –
    the trouble bringer
    the soother
    the enigmatic ones.

For now though all lie
enfolded
and in the black cauldron
no finger stirs.

But don't presume the day will dawn
like other days
or light will break revealing
the face in which, last night,
you went to sleep.

In her womb you may imagine
the storm wind waking,
or the soft one that will not lift a hair.

You do not know
and that is what she counts on.

    Look at the clouds
boiling up out of the pit,
feel on your face
the paws of the rain.

## TOWER OF THE WINDS

Weathered
the stone wind gods
are learning to fly,
their drapery hangs
on chipped shoulders,
their hair loosens.

    They are becoming
the wind and light and rain . . .
There, in the barley field,
waves & eddies,
forms enfolded and released,
shape-shifters,
       currents of fresh air.

## WRITING IT

That almost non-existent –
the thing you cannot see –
which might be everything,
you can't be sure,
you have no word –

or call it universe,
elusive light
in veins of leaf and wing,
the fingers of your hand.

## TO A WOMAN WITH A SUNFLOWER

Here are two faces
side by side, one smiling
for the warmth that fills both.

Dearest, no one draws you down
to the cruel and narrow place
that was your childhood once.

It is not I alone who call you back.
It is these faces shining
full with the light of the sun.

## SELF-PORTRAIT WITH FALLING LEAVES

1

After long stillness
a breath
which the wind-chimes felt

Night music
and a rattling house.

2

Dawn in a shower of colour,
wind ragging the nest of the woods.

What I love though
are the countless differences
words point to, but cannot catch:

a boat rocking on air
an arrow gliding
wings that turn or float or drift
this slow one downing that would love to climb
the other quick as a bird:

a leaf, and another leaf

each itself, but all it seems
one – a fall
that lays open the heart of the wood

this circular flight which seems
for a moment
endless

## NOT THE NEW POETRY

A blackbird pecking
an apple left hanging
on the tree – a red apple
with a white cap of snow.

It's like nothing in the world
but another blackbird
landing on another branch
which quivers, shedding
a little snow.


## OWLS CALLING ON A WINTER NIGHT

which to the listener
sleepless in his bed
sounds like 'Where, where?'
and an answering 'Here, here'.

But who knows, who knows,
silence returning
with a fever of human fears.


## SNOW LIKE THOUGHT

because it arrives
seemingly from nowhere
small flakes wandering
sideways
down & up & down

then faster, heavier

bringing up
deeper silence
from some place not dreamed of
that was always there.

# IMAGE-MAKER

### 1

Enku chipped images
from cypress wood –
a monk with a hatchet
deftly shaping
a thousand Buddhas.

He carved an earth god
from a chopping block.
He cut spirits of magic
and of fire from living wood.

### 2

It was not craft alone
that made him, but passion
to become passionless.

Discipline sent him out
to brave demons,
and shape himself.

He venerated the gods
of many places, and moved on.

### 3

He travelled far,
fulfilling his vow to make
one hundred thousand images:
bird-god and dragon-king,
guardian of the hearth,
protector of children,
god of poetry,
god of happiness.

His deity was Sacred Kannon,
the one who listens.
As he listened, observing
all needs, all expressions,
and deftly carving them.

Enku, keeper of the shrine,
moved on, complete
with emptiness.

## TO A MAKER OF LIGHT OBJECTS

The clouds inform you,
particles are your teachers,
you know what it is to float –
enwombed seed.

The light that set out from stars
billions of years ago,
spaces within atoms,
all the lights that elude us
but of which we can say
if we could see them
they would look
        something like this.

# A DIFFERENCE OVER THE STARS

'Cold things,' she says,
shuddering at the memory
of such black distance,
stars like cracks in ice on a pond.

But to him they are a blaze
in his young mind, far off now
but a warmth he comes back to,
face ruddy with firelight,
sparks swarming
under the roof of the sky.

## BUTTERFLY CLOUD

After days without a breath
still and hot
the white buddleia stirs,
wings open, whirr, tremble,
and cloud –
Atlantic cloud,
white cloud – moves
with a sea of fresh air
into opening sky

## BUTTERFLY EXTRAVAGANZA

Hairstreak of light, speckle
under orchard trees . . .
something's taking shape,
outside, within.
    Then the day begins
to turn, spinning,
scattering light –
red  pearl  brimstone  green –
a blur, illegible.
You catch at words, you say:
admiral – fritillary – tortoiseshell
but each is a hook that will not hold.
    Suddenly
there are eyes everywhere,
and the sun's power pulsing
in millions of veins.
Afterwards the air is still,
restless  Do not trust a leaf.
You fall asleep, and dream,
or maybe wake, seeing
the perfected form:
a purple emperor sailing
high over oaks, escaping.
Opening your eyes, you catch
the day emerging, unfolding
broad, blue wings.

## BARLEYFIELD WIND

Midsummer wind,
thought across the mind:

a running hare,
invisible, a hare-shape –
gone – leaving the field
motionless, supple,
greeny yellow. Ripple,
current, eddies,
whirlpool, a pattern created
and in one movement unmade . . .

Quiet then quick,
a country undiscovered,
mapped, unknown.
It is all imagination:
pooling – running – streaming –
a long, slow surge.
Then, barely a touch,
the whiskered heads
brushed by a breath.
And all the time,
burnishing every grain,
the sun brings to fruition:
a dry, brittle gold.

## THE BRAMLEY AT MOOR FARM

Old trunk,
iron-rooted, bowed,
how delicate the shadow
of your leaves upon the grass.

1

This is the hazel nut
the squirrel did not want:

an empty house
charcoaled with decay

the devil's granary
the evil eye

2

The scarecrow skull
sits grinning on its pole,

the north wind blows,
the rag-coat pockets fill with snow.

## GREEN WINTER SPRING

*(On receiving the gift of a David Tress landscape)*

The word that sprang to my lips
was *nesh* – tender-fresh,
with a hint of the chill that kills.

But this is alive, and wild –
celandine yellow
springing from brown earth, black earth,
new leaves again, pushing the dead aside.

Little flower, rising
from layered earth to meet the sun
through turbulent cloud – clouds
storming the Pembrokeshire hills.

Earth too is beginning to cloud,
a little green, a little yellow,
black and brown with masses of white.
Limbs in the hazel copse ache with returning life.

The word is quick on my tongue.
Sun pierces layer on layer,
coming to rest in the face of a flower.

That noise at dusk –
a bat squeak
or the high faint shriek
of gods emptying
themselves into the void.

\*

The ocean of being
moves on the ocean
of nonbeing
into which it falls
drop by drop.

## ELUSIVE LIGHT

Mind on pathways
through hidden landscapes
imagines the secrets
by which it exists

cloudscape
smoke dance
light
      flickering

## ORPHEUS

The truth is,
after the bold descent,
the song calling,
echoing,
he was absorbed
    into the ground.

Eurydice,
tendrils twined
around him,
climbed up
the ladder of his bones.

## ORPHIC FRAGMENTS

Song journeys
from mouth to mouth

tundra to tundra
on foot, with horse & mule & ox

over water, by log boat & sail
from coasts of China & Japan

north to the Arctic
south to the Pacific

crossing borders
light to dark to light

words mixed
with saliva & blood

one song journeying
in countless tongues

*

Eurydice
very Eurydice
gone

*

The world I left to seek her
was the world she kindled,
fire that is the very life in things

Her voice pierced me
and echoed everywhere.

And she is only a feather,
a curl of dust?

I will not say what I saw was only a phantom.
Can I say I lost in turning more than a dream?

*

Out of this world there is another nature
no one can speak of.

Over the border the dark
is not night nor the shadow mist.

You cannot say 'tree' or 'flower'.
No word conjures substance or shape.

Tell me, then, what is the use of poetry?

I could answer: poetry gives the rowers
the rhythm of the stroke
and when the sea roars, soothes it,
charms the rocks and lulls the dragon to sleep.

This I can brag of, but what I desired most
no word could deliver.

And so I sing.
And my words fill with emptiness.
And longing becomes my song.

## ON LOOKING INTO A WAY OF LIFE

'... in a world rocked by greed, misunderstanding and fear, with the imminence of collapse into unbelievable horrors, it is still possible and justifiable to find important the exact placing of two pebbles.'

JIM EDE

in and out of the paintings
          in and out of the rooms
the way of the maker leads
round and round
                    pebble
by pebble
shell by shell
              circling
              tracing with the mind's fingers
grain of wood
bowl & jug
fisherman's glass ball

shadow takes hold among the things
light plays silent notes

'the joy of opening windows'
the joy of closing them
              the maker's face
reflected in painted glass

outside – the sea

still energy
from savaged hands
'something of transparent peace'

instant made to last

feather-light
on massive swell
the boat
       this man's life
risen in his mind
bedded in his flesh
come to rest
where the spirit's hand moves
round and round

in living space
           in and out

# FRIEND WITH A SUNBURST

*For Jim Insole on his seventieth birthday*

Call it a shield, a boss, an image
of the wheeling sun. Call it
what you will, but I say
this is miracle also.

How it shines!

In fact, something of earth,
where water and fire have met,
and mind and heart, quick
in the hand moulding the clay,
letting the image form,
mastering the flaming sun.

I'm amazed at the burst of it:
creation contained in an image –
an old story
new as the first time told, colours
fresh with the maker's kiss.

Call it also a gift that rings
with his song – a world
played into being, hand and heart
and voice at one.

How it flames but does not burn.
How it bursts but does not break.

Call this also a gift for friendship's sake:
a form that kindles, and sustains –
a shield, a boss, an image of the wheeling sun.

---

* Jim Insole's sunbursts are embossed and decorated ceramic plaques
embodying the artist's religious vision.

## COCKLER

*(After an early Lee Grandjean sculpture)*

There are materials to work with –
elmwood, oil paint –
and he is young, experiencing
a new life at the edge –
with joy, and passion to work.

Thoughts come, ideas
of reinventing the human figure.
But what is thought
without a body to feel with,
or a sense of what the body is part of?

Watching people on the beach
he sees a man gathering cockles,
a man in shirt sleeves, trousers rolled.

And what he sees is energy –
power grips the man's shoulder
and the bucket he holds
which drips and swells.

With energy, he renders what he sees
in elmwood and paint –

a man jagged with fire, connected
to the sand where he scrabbles,
groping for cockles with an electric hand.

# 4 GOD'S HOUSES

## ST FAITH'S, LITTLE WITCHINGHAM

Ground elder, nettles, red campion
a semi-circle of lime trees,
island among Norfolk fields.

Inside, we step into emptiness
a familiar musty smell
sunlit white walls. Here though
how dramatic the fragments of story –

a man's leg twisted violently
as he braces himself to deliver the scourge,
a ladder, placed as it might be
against a house wall, to bring down the body from the cross.
Thomas feels with his fingers for the wound.

Such violent action
drawn with delicacy
and gentleness, so that, almost,
we can see the hand moving with the brush
scrolling vine leaves,
rounding a grape, touching in
the forked, red beard.

Nothing is missing
though so much has gone.

Only plague finished the work
leaving life in this empty decommissioned shell.
Soon grass will be at the windows,
leaf shadows move with the vines,
ground elder, nettles, red campion
rise up to bury the nameless stones.

Inside, a quick hand brushes the walls.

# CATHEDRAL

'The greatest error of historical Christianity is linked with the fatally limiting idea that the revelation is finished, and that nothing more is to be expected, that the building of the Church is completed and the roof laid on it.'

NICOLAI BERDYAEV

1

True: we can see
what must happen.

As the raft of logs rotted
on which the stone ark was built,
so this too will founder,
and return, past
the mason's marks,
to some jumble of stone.

All pomp, all history,
all lies and half-truths,
both boasts and gentle memorials,
marks of the meek, signs
of the mighty,
every kept bone,
each pinch of dust,
all of it, gone.

So we may imagine,
who won't be here to see.

And wind picking over
crumbled earth
and some jumble of stone

as wind picks over
the Giant's Ring on Salisbury Plain.

2

But this is different,
you could say.

We know the story;
it won't be lost.

Images,
electronic images,
will probably remain.

How should that matter
to a heart that hungers,
to a creature
with a passion for prayer?

What survives, then,
but a sense of incompletion?

And a people who are poets
at the core – who expect.

They will stand wondering
in this place, feeling
wind picking over
ground where the building stood,
dissolved like cloud.

They will come with questions
they seek to answer.

Questions that are themselves.

## ST BARTHOLOMEW'S, WINCHESTER

*In memory of Elizabeth Bewick*

Most of this place lies underground –
Old Minster, New Minster,
Hyde Abbey, dissolved.

Site then of a bridewell, where
prisoners labouring with mattock and spade
threw up bones, broke open
a coffin, sold the lead –
as men will, who need to live.

We, too, met over broken things,
a marriage, a beloved friend
whom you'd cared for, dead.
In your cottage by the church
we talked, discussed poems, shared our grief.

They are digging there now,
near the plot where your ashes lie,
finding, perhaps, a bone of Alfred
or his son, but digging, always digging.

There were books here a thousand years ago,
a Bible, a *Liber Vitae* picturing
a monk holding an open book
inscribed with names of a company
copied by God in heavenly pages.

You loved the old building
where you worshipped, close
to your home, the grassy plot
with a few trees, a thrush singing.

Yours too was a book of life.
You were a love poet in old age,
a poet in sickness and in health,
even in hospital, when you nearly died.

Only death would stop you seeking
the words, the rhythm,
the exact emotional shape.

And now your ashes have joined
the detritus of centuries,
where everything is history,
archaeology, digging, digging,
reading fragments of bone.

It is a place littered
with broken things,
but you are no part of these.

On the stone path,
pausing among the tombs,
I hear your words, and feel your spirit,
which is never still.

## HOLY ROOD, SOUTHAMPTON

1

November, 1940:

I am safe,
or not so safe,
in the womb.

Not far off,
people lie dead
or injured
in their wrecked homes.

On stormy seas,
danger overhead
and in the deep,
seamen venture out.

2

As the smoke clears,
Holy Rood is open,
windowless, a wreck.

3

And now, with black flukes
of a great anchor fast in the nave,
it remains open: a memorial
to men of the Merchant Navy.

Nowhere holds me more
than this space open to the gulls
and wind that brings a tang
of salt to city streets,
a pause to the bustle.

Holy Rood: I bow my head.

## NETLEY

You would think these abbey ruins
the house of peace –
woods and water embowering
grey stone and shaven green;
all human purpose dissolved,
the ring of bells melted
into silence.
          Yet what Constable saw
was turbulence, fury –
a glimmer of white surrounded
by darkness, black birds
buffeted, blown about by a storm wind;
and, to the side,
a dark red figure.

Once seen, he will haunt you.
Who is he? What does he see?
His eyes perhaps are filled with ruins,
the smashing of images,
the choir silenced,
the body of the house emptied,
broken, its materials carted off
or left to decay.

And perhaps he sees too
the ruins that will come,
armies gathering on the water,
ships returning with the wounded,
and, through the trees,
across the water, the city burning.

1

It was the churchyard where gorse ends,
dug from the Common,
our playground,
once known as Donkey Town –
not in our time, though
cattle and ponies strayed in
from the Forest, and, yes,
now and then a donkey or two.

Neighbours lie there now.

In old age, the rows
of white stones horrified my father,
though by then he could see them
only in his mind.

2

At Evensong the bells
called me down, past the gorse
and grazing cattle, past
the pond that was usually dry.

I loved especially the words
'troublous life' on the parson's lips.

'O Lord, support us all the day long.'

3

What little devils we were,
snorting in our hymn books
at suspicion of a fart,
turning *pilgrim* to *grimpil* . . .

But it was there solemnity claimed me.

Shining brass plaques with heroic names.
Language rolling among the pews

like sea in a cave, and above all
my father singing,
his voice raised above all the rest.

## ST AGNES, CAWSTON

1

A child would see them
fearfully in his mind,
and cry out for light.

He would hear creak
of wooden wings beginning
to move, and see
unforgiving faces
set towards – what?

In the dark they would swoop,
silent as vampire bats.

2

I am not a child now
to be afraid of the dark,
or should not be.

Nor is it fear that draws me
across the fields
to the stone tower
familiar of pheasant and hare
and the white owl
that hunts along the beck.

3

House of carved angels
that stand like trees in wind
on tiptoe at the brink of flight,

it is like a stone idol
beckoning,

a blunt statement
that says what it means.

## BOLDRE CHURCH REVISITED

My father and his cousin
painted this church,
companionable artists,
easels among the tombs,
each with his vision
of aged brick and stone,
red against grey,
the tower on the hill,
New Forest woods below.

He gave the painting to the school
which I attended, close by,
where I began to know myself
a little: a fond, foolish boy.

One Christmas, stiff
with fright, I read a lesson,
my Hampshire burr carrying over.

Older, the Hood Chapel
drew me in, imagining
lives torn apart, walls shaken,
the peace of this quiet place
exposed; as, of course, it was not.

Reminiscence tempts –
a recital of decomposed memory
sprouting half-truths,
ways of the little self,
a bubble of identity,
the whole river
that powers on, forgotten.

It was a day in spring,
the first drowsy bumblebee
humming past, daffodils
and primroses on the banks,
when we scattered my father's ashes
on the river below. I saw briefly
a whitish smear sinking
in opaque depths as the current
bore them down and away.

Above ancient oaks
with the first hint of leaf,
the church stood out,
red against grey.

There was nowhere
I could think of he would rather be.

## ST ISSUI, PATRISHOW

Into the Black Mountains,
raised to the sky,

buzzard cry, kronk
of a raven below

narrow lane toiling up, past
Nant Mair and holy well

past the stone where Giraldus
came with Bishop Baldwin

preaching the Third Crusade
into the small church

with beautiful carved oak
rood loft and screen –

what's this, or should I say who!
Mr Death, I presume,

hands full with hour glass
and scythe, a spade

hung from his arm.
Not today, mister.

From the porch, stone
floor splashed with dung

see mountains and sky,
in a mud nest over head

swallows, little faces
looking out, eager to fly.

## ST BRYNACH, NEVERN

1

This was the magic west.

A bloody site
of raiding and slaving.

A place of learning,
of men familiar with Arthur
and Dewi Sant.

Brynach was an Irishman
who talked with angels.

2

Knotwork,
an old order
at the hand of man.

Memorials in ogham and Latin.
And stones, stones, stones –

High Cross,
old tombs and stones
newly inscribed.

What wealth,
what a jumble.

On top of it all
a yew tree that bleeds.

God knows
who will make sense of it!

*With thoughts of T. F. Powys*

1

Muck on country lanes,
good dirt,
and fields of Blackmoor Vale
and distant Bulbarrow.

A place where a man
might hide himself from the world.

This, however, was a man
on no map known to us
though he chose to live here,
close to the churchyard wall
communing with the dead.

His tomb is a stone book,
the last enigmatic page
given over to the grass.

2

Obliteration
was his word for death,
a final consignment
of all he was to silence,
a gift to God's Acre.

There is, perhaps, a mystery of the self
that reaches beyond the self,
a silence that deepens
beyond the word.

3

I have sat where he sat
in a pew of the empty church
listening, wondering
about this man.

I have followed his steps
on the Dorset lane,
smelling the good smell
of sun-warmed dirt,
watching skylark and peewit
over fields towards Bulbarrow,
entranced by tiny things,
grass seed and celandine,
ditches humming with summer.

I have read his words
and thought at times
I glimpsed a mind I might know.

But each time he escaped
as perhaps he too, listening
for the dead beyond the wall
escaped from himself, reaching
into depths he could not fathom.

## SALISBURY CATHEDRAL:
## THE BUST OF RICHARD JEFFERIES

'I look at the sunshine and feel that there is no contracted order:
there is divine chaos, and, in it, limitless hope and possibilities.'
RICHARD JEFFERIES

1

What is this man –

sad-eyed, with a beard
birds could nest in
if it weren't marble?

They brought him in
out of the wild,
refashioned him:
a Victorian worthy,
with a niche in the habitat
of bishops, burghers, and knights –

this man who disliked churches,
who found spires poking up
from cornland and downs
an offence,
who wished ruin on temples.

2

Would he seek refuge here today?

On Liddington Hill
he would hear the M4
and smell the fumes.
At Coate Water, estates move in.

Or say Wild England lives
where he knew it, in ditch
and field corner, where
I have seen it with his eyes?

3

If there has to be a statue
let it be one a bird can shit on,
something one can imagine
feeling the wind –

as I felt the wind blowing
through his words,
breaking images,
leaving knowledge
a heap of ruins, driving me
back from the known.

4

There are words
that scatter dead languages,
words that break
statues and statutes
that hide what is real.

This man walked out
of the life prepared for him,
smashed the marble forms.

He opened himself to chaos.
He lived by the quickest word.

It will not be petrified
by this absurdity.

Listen to the wind rising
among the monuments,

preparing to scatter them
like pieces of eggshell and leaves.

# KNOWLTON

### 1

Like images of sun or moon
the circles spread out
on Cranborne Chase.

This, the largest,
an earth-banked Neolithic henge,
embraces the ruined tower
of a Norman church – a place,
one imagines, re-sanctified,
with a congregation
Black Death carried off.

On some nights
ghost-hunters haunt
the empty shell, with a company
of bats, and sometimes an owl.

The Devil carted off
the bell they listen for.

### 2

You, my dear,
on a journey with me
over ancestral ground,
on a sweet day in June,
smell blood and hear cries.

'Take me home,' you say.

I hear only birds among the corn.

Should I see ghosts,
they would be our kin,
men and women labouring
bent-backed in rich fields
between circles,
among ancient burials.

## ABBEY DORE

Usually I come here
mainly for one thing:

most golden
in all the Golden Valley

a head lying
among fragments

a shining face
plump as a cherub's

a mischievous smile
foliage around the lips

like muttonchop whiskers . . .

Today, though, scents
also draw me in

honey of lime leaves
orchard blossom

where cloisters were
and among the grass

down on their knees
three old, arthritic rams.

How fitting that this
should be their home

after a lifetime
of begetting,

descendants of flocks
on which the abbey was built.

Fitting, too, that the Green Man
boss indeed

among broken things
should, with scent

of lime leaves,
and three old rams,

come into his own.

# KILPECK

### 1

Allt-yr-Haul,
Hatterall Hill,
this 'wooded slope of the sun'.

Border country
where names are exchanged

where nature springs from human loins
and all is creative flux.

### 2

All praise to the master
with strength and delicacy in his hands
imagination at the tips of sense

knower of man and woman
falcon and deer, fish dog and boar

God's creatures, his inventions
all wrought in the web
figures of high art,
sculpted

dreaming magical dreams
monsters
beast tongues
bursting buds.

### 3

Falcon and deer, fish dog and boar
creatures of the chase,
quarry of lords

who harried this land,
masterful men
who grasped creation in their hands.

4

All praise to the maker
of sculpted forms,

of woman as the mouth of hell,
ravening cunt,
mother of the myriad forms.

5

And who were his masters
if not masterful men

lords of the chase,
castle-builders, drivers

of men and women
who slaved in these fields,

who lay down at last
with falcon and deer

with oxen in the red soil,
flesh blood and bone

builders of the border
under Allt-yr-Haul,

Hatterall Hill,
this 'wooded slope of the sun'.

## EGLWYS HYWYN SANT, ABERDARON

'astronaut / on impossible journeys / to the far side of the self'
                                    R. S. THOMAS, 'The New Mariner'

A saint without a story –
we may imagine him,
Saint Hywyn,
in the stone church beside
the stone beach, watching
seas break on the sacred island,
committing his prayers
to the airways and the waters,
faithful to the evidence
of things not seen.

A man we do not know
A man we may imagine.

ili

Centuries pass.

Another man's shadow
falls on the rocks.

At once the creatures scatter,
grey seals dive, seabirds
rise clamouring,
even the little warblers,
fellow passengers,
that he loves to glimpse, vanish.

He is alone, in touch
with the earth's crust,
scholar of faults and fractures,

a man launching his mind
on the darkness that surrounds him,
and on the darkness within.

*

Where are the poets?

He sniffs the air,
not an ogre, rather
a stag scenting the air
for a rival.

Where are the poets?
Dead with the saints,
with the farmers
and fisher folk?

Is the new language
an air too thin to breathe?

There is an old tongue
that the saints and poets preached,
and the creatures heeded,
and God, perhaps, abided.

Is he, as he stands here
casting his shadow
on the rock, launching
his probes, the last poet?

*

Lord, forgive
your poets their pride.

Even the greatest,
the man on the stone beach,
is a frail craft,
a stuttering probe,
an obstructed channel
giving shape to a drop
of the life that made him.

*

Be sure of this.

We have heard his voice.
It will not be unheard.

We have looked with his eyes.
What he has seen
will colour our seeing.

His shadow will remain
on the ancient rocks.
Pilgrims will come
seeking to know his story.

They will imagine him
committing his prayers
to the airways and the waters,
probing the darkness
that is now, because
of him, more nearly their own.

## ST BRIDE'S, LLANSANTFFRAED

1

Two stone heads –

little else remains
from the building he knew,
HENRICUS VAUGHAN SILURIS.

Neither he nor his brother
would recognise their church,
Henry and Thomas,
poet and alchemist
for whom 'God's building'
was 'full of Spirit, quick, and living'.

2

A yew tree
and a green-stained
lettered slab of stone.

Moles working
in the dust and clay
he knew himself to be.

What is his boast?
What is his gift?
PECCATOR MAXIMUS.

3

This, though, is not a place of memory.

Light tracks the Brecon Beacons,
lies in pewter pools
or flashes silver, sudden
blinding falls along the Usk.

The very air is quicker for his breath.

# 5  ISLAND VIEW

ISLAND VIEW

*for Mimi Khalvati*

Chert by flint
            the pebbled bank
sheer stone
            and across the water –
turbulent sea-lanes,
warships, ocean liners,
jungles of kelp & wrack –
West Wight and the Needles
haloed in light,
                another world.

Breakwaters
of Portland stone,
fragments of abbey ruins,
remains of a concrete pillbox,
ages jumbled
forming a solid wall.

And much though I wish it
I hear no whisper through,
no voice that is not the sea's,
sibilant, sibylline . . .

'But they're nothing like needles,'
he said, my brother,
lying beside me on Barton beach.
'Why don't they call them the pins?'
That was the time he instructed me how to fly,
by instrument, in cloud.
All in imagination, of course, by word of mouth.

When Mother died, six weeks before him,
I scattered her ashes there.

And I would say this today: Show me
the breakwater's hardest stone, iron bolts
that salt corrodes, bleeding
in splintered wood, cliff-falls,
landslides of blue clay
obliterating paths.
                    Show me all this
and I would see through it,
and find a man laughing,
leaning on his elbow on the sand.

## SALTGRASS LANE

1

Blank as a sheet of paper
the mud shines
as the tide ebbs.

Shines blankly
before the gulls come
and the waders, piping.

Would it be the same
if I could go back
and lie down on rough grass
watching sun-lit cloud
on a September day
passing and never-ending?

2

All the world here
that isn't water is stone.

Stone and mud,
and fleshy, salt-loving plants.

Water mirrors
waders and gulls
as the tide ebbs, draining
sky from the estuary.

Now I climb the shingle-spit,
slide back, scramble over.

Over the bank the sea meets me

with a smack of light,
colour and salt-lashed air.

Behind me the lane ending at the bridge
creeps away, silver-grey as snail shine
back the way I came.

3

For an old man
who walks with difficulty
memory is to return
without a stumble.

Feet springing on the lane,
feet hanging over the bridge
where he dangles a rind
on a string weighted with a stone.
Crabs in the murk wave their claws.
The day is tense with expectation.

Legs striding, legs at ease,
body unconscious
as a fish or a bird.

4

Tern's wing and curve
of shingle-spit,
gull and lighthouse:
white echoes white at high tide
on the water's mirror.

Days, though, are visible fractions,
so many pictures shattering.
Power unabated works unseen,
sun quickening water and plant –
thrift & sea-purslane & horned-poppy.

Sand waves drive through,
clouds of sediment settle,
tides mould, unmake, remould . . .

Underwater, a wreck's ribs are unpicked,
currents swirl, abrade, scour,
among detritus, in nutrient dark,
algae and larvae replenish the multitude.

A father watching his son pick up a stone
sees, momentarily,
a vision of power –
the boy hurling the beach into the sea.

5

Legs with little power
and each word a stumble,

a slippery step

plunging in cracks & creeks,
squeezing out prints
of mineral-rich, polluted ooze.

Drawing a line that runs out,
finding a foothold
on a surface scribbled over:
hieroglyph, palimpsest

            *mewl   pipe   cry*

Or as ducks dabble,
or dunlin follow the ebb.

Step feeling after step
each word composing,
decomposing, moving on.

6

Everything here speaks of defences –

a castle built in part from abbey stone,
the concrete shell of a pillbox,
breakwaters, shingle
built up by longshore drift.

One yellow horned-poppy,
apparently with no soil to root in,
stands up between sea and castle walls.

7

I do not expect to walk here
alive again.

Nor do I wish to come
only in memory
repeating taken steps.

Or as some living phantom
who walks without touching
and the blind reaching of touch.

This was always somewhere between,
with no beginning or end,

always a place in the making
where I was happy to be.

8

As well ask the stones
who he is, the man who wanders
in and out of time –
friend and lover,
brother, father, son.

As soon ask sand and shells
which the tide covers and uncovers,
shifting them, breaking
one seeming pattern
to leave another
which the next flood breaks.

As well question the trunk
skinned white
cast up with feathers & corks.

Or the clothes left on the beach.

Naked,
he is not the one you seek.

9

On the crown of the bank
against the sky
a man and a woman walk away

small figures at a distance
between saltmarsh and sea.

Step by step
they move away,
hand in hand.

Soon there will be nothing to see,
and what you will have seen
is nothing, not a jot
of the sea they see, nothing
of sun kindling the stones
they tread on, or kiss
of salt on eyelashes and lips.

Nothing but the distance
in which they vanish,
into the world they have made
between them, where they walk away.

10

Flounders and small green crabs
are working in the mud,
bass swimming in with the tide.

Sure-footed, I stand
on slippery stones.

Gull islands, wallowing
as the tide returns,
begin to disappear,
washed smooth and shining.

## BATH STONE

'We may think of ["The Ruin"] as the first of many English
meditations on old stones.'
MICHAEL ALEXANDER, *The Earliest English Poems*


First the water, but how
separate the water
from the stone
                    Fosse Way
from Jurassic seas


        Remember
the old men working –
picker, chopper, sawyer
monumental masons,
architects
whose elegant visions
clothe the hillsides


Think of the horses working
underground, hauling waggons
loaded with blocks of stone –


        Punch
depicted tenderly
on the wall of a stone mine
by a haulier's hand


Remember also the builders
of tholos and temenos,
the sculptor of a cavalryman
trampling enemies of Rome
under his horse's hooves

      whose steps do you hear
at night ringing on paving-stones
where you pass a boy sitting
in a shop doorway, shivering
with his dog lying beside him

His head droops as you pass –
      does he feel a way down
in the long hours, city
under city, where
warm waters lap him round

How nimbly stone angels
over his head mount
rung over rung

How glassily windows
under the neon-lit
dome of cloud
stare

At this hour the streets
are empty, the last guided tour
put to bed, not a rustle
of a ballgown
not a coin or curse
offered – waking – to the gods

      Think of them, the first
to penetrate to the source,
pushing through a tangle
of roots and branches,
drawn by the steam, the smell,
the prey

who found gore
splashed on boulders
who imagined in the boiling
black mud a face

      Listen:
in the sound of acid rain
you can hear the end
speaking to the beginning,
lead pipes echoing the voice
of water gushing from underground,
water that speaks the language
of ancient rain, that seeped down,
heated at the earth's core
emerged under pressure
at fault-lines
                    here

Approach as close as you dare
the imagined place
worked and reworked
built over, again fallen in
shaped stones
shattered
red tiles broken

where a poet stands,
                wondering

## STRAWBERRY LAND

1

First, the old smell,
salt on the air, brings back
the river, mud-banks, shingle
thatched with weed and straw.
Crabshells. Tarred feathers.

A black-headed gull –
one is enough to transport you
over the river onto a gravel hard,
a caved-in concrete path,
which leads to a lane
between strawberry fields.

It is all a mixture of water,
soil and air – boats
and flying boats,
Tiger Moths that are falling leaves,
Swordfish drawing shadows
over the fields.

A boy with a sticky, red mouth
looks up from where he lies
concealed between rows, tasting
a sweetness that will be mixed,
always, with sun-warmed dust,
the sharpness of gravel patterning
bare legs and arms.

He tastes words, too,
from which he will build a world:

> shore
> > flotsam
> > > gull
> punnet
> > strawberry
> > > cloche.

2

This was my mother's country.

I think she would know it still
for all the change – the Hamble River,
visible among the yachts,
where once, she said, at high tide,
a whale ventured upriver
as far as Botley, and ran aground.
Tall tale, I said, uncertainly,
mixing history with myth.

She would know the names:
Swanwick, Bursledon, Park Gate.
Sarisbury Green, where she married,
and her mother and father are buried.

I see her by the shore and in the fields,
a girl, a young woman picking strawberries,
a mother with a child.

She would laugh at the ferry:
a shock of pink called *Emily*,
her grand-daughter's name.
From Hamble to Warsash
it weaves among yachts

whose names she would relish:
*Discovery, Artemis, Valhalla,*
*C'est moi* – fibreglass
at moorings where once
*Little Jesus* rode, and *Holy Ghost.*
And hapless *Grace Dieu,*
a warship without a war,
her majesty leaking at a mud-berth,
lightning-struck, left to rot.
As boats we thought Viking
rotted in ooze, shells
of blackened oak,
a perch for a heron or a gull,
an excuse for a story
part fable and part truth.

3

Gull cry, *tink-tink*
of steel on alloy,
flap of canvas
as a sail is raised
*perkle – perkle – perkle,*
engine of a wooden boat –
one for you, which you liken
to an old-fashioned
coffee percolator.

Listen: we are composing
the day between us, mingling
our voices with the sounds.
Or say we are a small part
only – which is true –
like sails reduced to pieces

of white butterfly wing
by the breadth of the waterway
and the shadow of Fawley
which speaks of power
with its moon city
and tongue of leaping flame.

4

From the edge of the Common,
among salt-loving plants,
where gun-emplacements
keep the memory of centuries of wars,
the shore appears dingy.

                      But step out
towards the water line,
where the tide has receded,
and what you find is like a palette
webbed stickily with yellows, purples,
reds, bright green.

Webbed, yet each thing distinct:
clam shell, barnacled pebble,
lugworm cast, brick fragment,
wracks, splinters of wrecks,
rags of red weed.

How rare it is, this place
of living colours,
how wonderful,
when you trust your feet
to the slippery foreshore,
and open your eyes.

5

A shingle shore
with a smell of salt,
the cry of a black-headed gull.

A strawberry field,
where a boy lies hidden,
red juice on his lips.

He will absorb
the stolen sweetness,
the mingled smells
of fruit and salt and dust,
the prints of gravel
sharp on his skin.

His words will taste of these things.

## HURST CASTLE

'It's very special how there are ways, a field, a place,
where our deepest creative concerns connect.'

NOAH PIKES

1

Dear friend,
you have sent my mind racing,
skipping the years.

2

You will know how the sea
runs up among the stones,
how it laps and lapses,
surges with the tide.
And wind whips off the foam.
And the Shingles buoy's bell rings.

Behind us, granite walls,
concrete, brick, rusted steel doors
clamped shut on cannon mouths.

A symbol of power,
once our playground,
empty as a cockle shell.

3

Somehow this place is a way.
I feel I can talk to you through the walls.

4

Remember the Franciscan priest
immured here for thirty years?

A poor, infirm man, one side
of his body palsied,
how he would shuffle
in a dark, narrow room,
the only human sound
his jailor's tread. Other voices,
the sea's whisper or breaking crash,
a gull's cry.

So news of a far world came to him,
free voices,
which spoke of imprisonment.

5

Who were his brothers then?
And how could he bless?

6

Your voice, dear friend, was choked for years,
unknown as a foreign tongue,
locked in the throat.

At last, released,
it spoke a name that was new to you,
your name,
with a force opening the body's dark and narrow space.

7

You take me back.
So many fields, cities, countries.
And this is the place you bring me to –

This way
of wood and brick defences,
old jetties, the granite castle
with its giant weight of wars
an empty cockle shell.

Words bring me, your words,
words we have spoken to each other,
that connect us to a world.

Outside this narrow room in which I write,
inside, penetrating the walls,
I hear voices that speak of the sea.